Table of Contents

4

A Simple Way to

END

POVERTY

in the United States

Dwight Clough

First, let us blame...

Democrats / Republicans
The Poor
The Rich
The Middle Class
Racism
Rotten parenting
Extra-marital sex
Laziness / Welfare
The breakdown of the family
Bungling bureaucrats
Idiotic government regulations
Evil corporations
Capitalism / Socialism
Indifference and apathy
Corruption
Greed and oppression
Addiction
Fill in the blank:

____

There.

Feel better?

So, let me ask you a question:

*How many people did we
release from poverty just now
by blaming?*

Ready to move on?

A thought experiment

I'm poor. Your job is to get me out of poverty in five years or less.

If you succeed, you get 100 million dollars.

If you fail, you will be shot.

Here are the rules: You can't just give me money; my ascent from poverty to the middle class and beyond must come from value I contribute, value fairly compensated.

Will you succeed?

Of course you will. Unless there's something seriously wrong with you, your desire to collect $100 million and escape the firing squad will motivate you to find a solution. You might not know how to help me, but you will find someone(s) who can.

Generational poverty is etched into the lives of its members, and there is no escape, right?

Wrong! If we really want to solve poverty, we can. One person at a time—we can.

But if we're going to get people out of poverty, we need to keep a few things in mind:

1. Everybody faces obstacles that must be overcome in order to succeed. By everybody, I mean Jeff Bezos, Bill Gates, the homeless guy you drove by yesterday, and you. These obstacles are both external an internal. If we don't find a way to overcome the obstacles, we're stuck. And the obstacles look a little different for each person. You won't get anybody out of poverty without helping

them identify and overcome obstacles.

2. Everybody needs help. By "everybody" I mean Warren Buffet, Donald Trump or Joe Biden (take your pick), the drug addict in the detox center, and you. Nobody—hear me—nobody succeeds on their own. Nobody does. You didn't. They didn't. Nobody does.

3. Maybe we can stop thinking of poor people as stupid, oppressed, lazy, morally deficient, or whatever, and start thinking of them as people just like you who haven't yet received the help you received to overcome the obstacles they face.

4. Here's a startling thought. Maybe we could actually get to know, like, and *respect* a few people living below the poverty line.

I will pause here to share a little story. I was driving and came to a stoplight one day, and there in the grassy median was a homeless woman, on her knees, staring down at the grass, the very picture of dejection.

I rolled down my window. "I'm sorry," I said, "I don't have any money,[1] but I just wanted to ask how you're doing."

She came over and we talked for a bit. Then the light turned green, and I needed to move on.

But before I did, she put her hand on my arm, looked me in the eye, and through tears she said, "Thank you for talking to me."

Thank you for talking to me.

---

1 Earlier that day I had given away the last of my money.

What's wrong with being human, with being kind, with treating people with respect?

5. Everybody is different. What works for you does not work for me. What works for me does not work for you. I'm not gonna try to turn you into a watered down version of me, and I will thank you not to try to turn me into a watered down version of you. Maybe instead we could focus on helping each other become the best version of ourselves.

6. Suppose we purge our culture of one of the worst ideas that ever permeated any culture. Here it is:

I must make you lose in order for me to win.

That's how we do politics. That's how we do journalism. That's often how we do business. That's sometimes how we do "friendship."

It pits rich against poor, Black against White, Republican against Democrat.

You must lose so I can win.

That's how our culture thinks. And it reeks. It's sick. But it's pervasive. That simple phrase encapsulates much of what is wrong in our world today.

Jim Rohn had a great line years ago: *"There's just one problem with trying to sink half the ship—guess what happens to your half!"*

Let's go back to our thought experiment. We don't have $100 million. And we're not going to put you up in front of a firing squad. So that idea is out.

But what could we do instead? If I'm poor, I don't have the money to pay you to help me get out of poverty.

And, sorry, no offense to you government people, but we don't want the government to pay you because the government doesn't know how to do anything without adding layers and layers of bureaucratic nonsense to it, and gumming up the works so much that by the end the only thing it does is keep a few government workers employed. (And, yeah, I used to work for the government.) The problem here is that the government is going to want to tell you how to do it, and one thing the government has clearly demonstrated over the last 50 years is this: They have no idea how to do it.

But maybe there's an in between solution, a creative alternative.

If you're nodding off, this would be a good time to get another cup of coffee because what I'm about to say is important.

Here's how it works:

I'm in poverty. As far as the government (or the taxpayer) is concerned, I'm a net liability. I cost money. Food Stamps. Medicaid. Earned Income Credit. Pell Grants. And so on.

You get me out of poverty. Look at what happened. The government (or the taxpayer) just got a double win.

Win #1. The government is no longer paying for Medicaid, Food Stamps, whatever. Big win.

Win #2. Now I'm paying taxes.

Now here's the proposal: What if the government gives Win #2 to you? You got me out of poverty. Here's your reward. The state and federal governments take the taxes they collect from me and turn them over to you. You just got a return for your investment in me.

Win win win.

The government (or taxpayer) wins. That's Win #1 described above.

You win because you get a return on your investment.

I win. I get out of poverty.

Here's the beauty of this. Other than the little bit of effort it takes to administer this, there's no new massive government programming that requires us to raise taxes, increase the deficit, mushroom the public debt. It's just a pass through. Money that's already there passes through to you.

In fact, this reduces government spending. Less money out for entitlements means more money for something else.

Let's review:

1. You help me out of poverty.

2. The government no longer buys welfare for me.

3. I start paying taxes.

4. The government collects those taxes and turns them over to you.

5. We all win.

I call this

Tax Diversion Financing™.

Is this idea bug free?

Probably not.

Will there be fraud?

Probably.

So here's what I suggest:

Test it with a pilot program. Do it on a small scale. Get the kinks out of it. Then roll it out nationwide.

Maybe there's a state out there that wants to try it in conjunction with the federal government. Why not give it a try?

Or, of course, if you don't want to do that, we can keep doing what we're doing...

We're currently locked in a battle between the Darwinists and the Robin Hoods. In my opinion, as a person who has lived much of my life below the poverty line, neither one has the solution. Let me explain.

And before you throw this book against the wall, please read both.

The Darwinists: Their mantra is "End the addiction."

Welfare keeps people in poverty, right? It breaks up the family. It robs dads of their dignity. It removes the incentive to work. People in generational poverty don't even know what work is.

Right?

As someone who has lived below the poverty line for much of my life,

as someone who has been on welfare,[2] I need to say, I agree.

To a point.

I'll be straight with you. I turned
down many opportunities to raise
my income by a little bit because I
knew I would lose more than I would
gain.

I could take the job[3] or the raise
or whatever, but then my family
loses Pell Grants, Food Stamps,
Medicaid, Earned Income Credit.

Do the math. It wasn't worth it.
Would you work twice as hard for
half as much?

If you answered yes, you're lying
—to me and to yourself.

---

2   Incidentally, did I just lose my credibility
    with you? And if so, why? What went on in
    your mind to make that happen?

3   In case you're wondering, I always worked.
    Often self employed, often working long,
    long hours for very little pay.

So welfare is the culprit, right? Just get rid of welfare, and then people will be motivated to go out and get a job and pull themselves out of poverty.

Yeah... About that... Getting rid of welfare may delight the Darwinist in you; you may see a great opportunity here for natural selection, for survival of the fittest, for weeding out the undesirables. They can starve on the side of the road waiting for an ambulance that never comes to take them to a hospital that won't receive them. Then you can finally burn their tent city.

Beautiful picture, isn't it?

I've been down to one meal a day, standing in a grocery store aisle with seventeen cents in my pocket staring at a can of beans for sixty-five cents that looked so good (but I couldn't afford it), wondering what I was going

to say to my four little children when
I got home.

Do you wanna try that?

I've been homeless with a wife
and a little baby, driving down the
highway in the city looking at all the
exits and realizing that none of them
are mine.

Do you wanna try that?

I was forced into bankruptcy trying to survive.

I've seen my wife in terrible pain,
and I was helpless to do anything.

Do you wanna try that?

You don't like welfare; I don't like
welfare, but welfare has a purpose.

You may not be a fan of morphine, but when you break a femur,
you just might change your mind.

The Robin Hoods: Their mantra, of course, is "Rob the rich, give to the poor."

I mean if a little morphine is good, then a whole lot more morphine would be even better, right? Morphine for everybody. Ten times a day morphine.

So let's put Robin Hood in charge. After all, the rich are evil, right? So let's let Robin Hood rob the rich and give to the poor.

Right...

Let's start by figuring out who Robin Hood is going to rob. Only those nasty rich people, right?

Not exactly. He won't tell you this, of course, but he plans to rob you.

If you make more than $30,000 a year, I got news for you: You are rich. Rich enough to get robbed by Robin

Hood. Yeah, yeah, yeah. I know he's promised, cross his heart, that he won't. But he will.

Believe me, he will.

And here's what you need to know: Robin Hood rapes as well as robs.

Robin Hood needs to rape. Pretty soon people figure out that Robin Hood is failing. It isn't working. So he needs someone to blame. Here are some popular choices: Jews. Christians. Blacks. Whites. Gays. Straights. (Your group hasn't come up yet? Don't worry, he will get around to you too.) All the Robin Hoods of the past—Pol Pot, Mao Zedong, Joseph Stalin, Fidel Castro (to name just a few)—there was a reason for their killing fields, their labor camps, their gulags, their underground torture chambers.

When Robin Hood finishes, no one will be rich except Robin Hood. Sure, his salary will only be $15,000 a year. But who needs a salary, when you have a dacha by sea, a chauffeur-driven limousine, a private jet, a team of servants, and caviar delivered to your suite.

Am I against the redistribution of wealth? Not exactly. I'm against letting Robin Hood do it.

And, look, Robin Hood doesn't just rob the rich. He also robs the poor. He robs them of their dignity. He robs them of the opportunity to make a living by making a contribution of value to their world. And he robs them of their escape route. He says to the poor: "If you prosper, if you escape poverty, then you become my enemy, and I will rob you."

I'm not saying that the rich don't have something the poor need. They do. But it's not money, precisely. It's something else. It's courage. It's confidence. It's connections. It's know how. It's purpose. It's knowing how to mine and market your own intrinsic value.

And if you Darwinists and Robin Hoods could just stop fighting for a moment and listen to a poor man, here's what I want you to know.

I don't want your programs. I don't want the bureaucratic nonsense you try to shove down our throats. I don't want to walk into your office and be greeted by an armed security guard.

I just want a friend. Someone who will listen without judging. Someone who will care, coach, encourage, empower, and cheer.

Why is that so difficult to understand?

I feel it's only fair to warn you that when good people start helping other good people get out of poverty, they're gonna wake up to the reality that the system sucks.

You're gonna have new voices calling on you to fix things that are broken. For starters, they're gonna figure out that the system itself is designed to keep people locked in poverty—that getting across that canyon from poverty to the middle class is daunting, and the system makes it harder.

This is partly because the system is designed to prevent welfare fraud; it's not designed to get people out of poverty.

So the system will need to change. But, hey, life is about change, right?

Let's embrace that.

PS. If you want to know where I'm coming from, you can watch my video here:

youtu.be/Hv-eAaUox5o